# THE SUNFLOWER FIELD

# THE SUNFLOWER FIELD

Written by: Kaitlyn A. Corsiglia
Illustrated by: Joseph Cowman

ELM HILL ®

A Division of
HarperCollins Christian Publishing

www.elmhillbooks.com

## The Sunflower Field

Published in Nashville, Tennessee, by Elm Hill, an imprint of Thomas Nelson. Elm Hill and Thomas Nelson are registered trademarks of HarperCollins Christian Publishing, Inc.

Elm Hill titles may be purchased in bulk for educational, business, fund-raising, or sales promotional use. For information, please e-mail SpecialMarkets@ThomasNelson.com.

**Library of Congress Cataloging-in-Publication Data**

Library of Congress Control Number: 2019906092

ISBN 978-1-400326242 (Paperback)
ISBN 978-1-400326259 (Hardbound)
ISBN 978-1-400326266 (eBook)

# Dedications and Acknowledgments

To Justin and my mom, Cassandra,
Thank you both for loving me and believing in all my
silly ideas! I am blessed to have both of you in my life.
You both push me to conquer my fears and without
either of you I would not be writing this story.

A special note to my dad, Thomas,
You gave me the ability to overcome my fears and to
be a strong-minded woman. In you I found the ability
to stand up for the things I want in life. Without you, I
wouldn't have figured out how to present ideas to
people and I sure wouldn't be the ice cream
loving girl you know today!

# THE SUNFLOWER FIELD

Sunflower – plants with large yellow-rayed flower heads
bearing edible seeds that yield an edible oil.

Family – Asteraceae (Aster Family)
Genus – Helianthus

It was a hot summer morning in July as Aster woke up smelling pancakes and syrup coming from the kitchen. Aster rolled over in bed and saw her calendar with a big red circle around today!

She knew what that meant, today was finally the day her mommy and daddy would take her to see the Sunflower Fields! Every year they had a countdown after Christmas to when they would go. This year was no different, except Aster's mommy and daddy had a secret surprise.

As Aster jumped out of bed, she remembered her mommy always told her to brush her teeth and wash her hands before breakfast. Aster raced to the bathroom and nearly scared herself as she saw her curly brown hair standing straight up on her head. She brushed her teeth in a hurry and raced down the hall to the kitchen!

When Aster reached the kitchen, her mommy was in her sunflower apron and covered in flour! Aster loved to see the sunflower-shaped pancakes and the bundle of sunflowers on the table. As she climbed into her chair and hollered, "Goooooooood morning!" her daddy jumped and laughed then replied, "Good morning, Aster. I think you have a bird's nest growing on your head!" He was always making fun of her hair, but that is probably because he is just jealous, seeing as he doesn't have any. As Aster was eating her pancakes, she caught Daddy spying over his newspaper at Mommy as she was singing and dancing all throughout the kitchen.

Every year around this time, Daddy would say to Mommy, "Thank you for planting that seed." Then he would whisk her off and start dancing in the kitchen and singing the sunflower song. Aster finished her pancakes in a hurry and then hollered at them, "I'm ready to go!

Mommy, can I wear my yellow dress today?"Her mommy replied, "Of course, sunshine, remember what I always say, though..." and before she could finish her sentence, Aster hopped off the chair and said, "'Remember the seed!' I know!"Aster raced Daddy to the car and of course she won. Aster needed help getting into the car, so he picked her up and put her in the car seat. "Daddy, I'm six now. I can buckle myself."He chuckled and said, "Of course, sunshine. Are you excited to see your surprise today?"She threw her arms around his neck to hug him and declared, "Can you tell me now, Daddy?"He got in the car and uttered, "As soon as we get to the Sunflower Field, I will tell you."

Aster was staring out the window when she saw a man working in a field like Daddy and asked, "What is that man doing? "Daddy replied, "He's a farmer, Aster." She thought real hard for a minute and then enquired, "Mommy, is Daddy a farmer like that man?"Mommy replied, "Your daddy works with plants."Aster thought real hard again until she blurted out, "Well then, what do you do, Mommy?" She answered, "I am a sower of seeds."

Daddy stopped the car and turned around to say, "We're here!" Before he could even finish, Aster yanked the car door open, letting the warm July air blow stray curls from her braids. The very same breeze would carry the sweet smell of sunflowers for miles. On days like today, where the sun is shining bright, the flowers seemed to smell even stronger.

Aster jumped down from the car and took off straight for the rows of sunflowers. Daddy caught up with her and threw her on his shoulders so she could see the miles of sunflowers. Aster tapped her daddy on the head and asked, "What is that big sign?"
He replied, "Let's go find out!" Aster's mommy was slow, so she always had to catch up with them.

Before Aster started to read the sign, her mommy handed her a sunflower seed. Her daddy helped her sound out the sign.

"Aster's ...... Sun ... flower ........ fi ... fild ... feld ..... fieeeeeld!

Aster's Sunflower Field!" She stopped and realized that her name was on the sign! "Hey, that's my name, right? My name's up there! Right? Right?"

"Yes, that is your name up there, Aster!" said her mommy. Aster laughed and jumped around with excitement until Daddy sat down on the bench by the sign and told her the surprise. As Aster sat with her listening cap on, Daddy and Mommy said, "Sometimes we plant seeds and are blessed to watch them grow. Other times we plant seeds and we don't get to see what happens next."

"Aster, you see all the flowers in this field? Well, sunshine, many years before you came along, Mommy and Daddy would come to this field and plant a sunflower seed every time we would talk to God about you," said Mommy. "The seed Mommy gave you," said Daddy, pointing to her hand, "is your seed to take home and watch grow! Then next year when we come back, you can plant your sunflower right here by your sign."

Mommy took Aster's hand as they started walking back to the car. Aster looked up at her mommy and exclaimed, "Remember my seed!" Mommy picked Aster up, kissed her forehead, and said, "Yes, ma'am! I'll never forget it."

When they got back home, Aster saw that Mommy was putting a yellow flower pot on the windowsill. So she ran over to find out what it was. "Just the little lady I was looking for," said Mommy, "Here is where you can plant your seed from earlier. We won't plant your seed until the day after Christmas though, okay?"

As the summer turned to fall and the fall turned to winter, Aster grew anxious to plant her seed. Their Christmas tree lights were shining bright on the beautiful yellow flower pot. As Aster stood gazing at the lights twinkling, her daddy came in the room with a piece of paper. Daddy joined Aster with a list and told her, "In order for the seed to grow into a sunflower, you have to remember it!"

As the winter came to an end, Aster and her flower grew. Her first sunflower bloomed just as summer was arriving....

"I remember it so clearly." Aster, who is now grown and with a daughter of her own, said. Emmy, Aster's daughter, sat staring at the window with a smile on her face. Aster finished telling her...,
"Don't forget the seed, sweetie. It's so important to tend to every seed, even the ones planted in our hearts. If you let the wrong seed take root, it can be a big mess to clean up later."

Just as Aster's parents planted sunflowers each time they spoke to God about her, Aster did the same thing with her husband Arthur. "Emmy, I want you to remember this story and teach your children about it one day as well," said Aster. "But Mommy, I still don't understand why you and Daddy are telling me this story?" said Emmy.

Aster's husband, Arthur, spoke up, "Sunshine, you're very special to us; we love you with our whole hearts. We are sharing this story because we have a little surprise." "What, Daddy! Tell me pleaseeeee!" Emmy said, excited. As Aster and Arthur stood together holding hands, they pointed to the pots on the windowsill and said, "You see this second sunflower pot, Emmy? Well, just as a seed grows in the soil, Mommy is growing a baby in her tummy."

With a shocked look on her face, Emmy shouted with joy, "What! Really? I'm going to be a big sister?" "Yes, ma'am, you are, and one day the three of us can teach your baby sister or brother all about remembering the seed and how to grow sunflowers."

And just like that, Aster smiled at her growing family and thought back to when she was Emmy's age. Aster's Sunflower Field flourished and brought happiness to their little town every year. Although she's grown, Aster never forgot what her parents taught her...
Never forget the seed!

# The End!

CPSIA information can be obtained
at www.ICGtesting.com
Printed in the USA
LVHW060341140819
627422LV00005B/23/P